J
394/2
GRI
    Griffiths, Jonathan
    New Zealand
    Festivals of the World

DATE DUE   10/99 $12.95

712-347-5492

Edward F. Owen
Memorial Library
1129 Willow Drive
Cart. Lake, IA 51510

DEMCO

Festivals of the World

NEW ZEALAND

Gareth Stevens Publishing
MILWAUKEE

Written by
JONATHAN GRIFFITHS

Edited by
GERALDINE MESENAS

Designed by
HASNAH MOHD ESA

Picture research by
SUSAN JANE MANUEL

First published in North America in 1999 by
Gareth Stevens Publishing
1555 North RiverCenter Drive, Suite 201
Milwaukee, Wisconsin 53212 USA

For a free color catalog describing Gareth
Stevens' list of high-quality books and multimedia
programs, call
1-800-542-2595 (USA)
or 1-800-461-9120 (Canada).
Gareth Stevens Publishing's Fax: (414) 225-0377.

© TIMES EDITIONS PTE LTD 1999
Originated and designed by
Times Books International
an imprint of Times Editions Pte Ltd
Times Centre, 1 New Industrial Road
Singapore 536196
Printed in Malaysia

Library of Congress Cataloging-in-Publication Data:
Griffiths, Jonathan.
New Zealand / by Jonathan Griffiths.
p. cm. — (Festivals of the world)
Includes bibliographical references and index.
Summary: Describes how the culture of New
Zealand is reflected in its many festivals and
celebrations, including Waitangi Day, the
Aotearoa Festival, and Golden Shears.
ISBN 0-8368-2033-9 (lib. bdg.)
1. Festivals—New Zealand—Juvenile literature.
2. New Zealand—Social life and customs—
Juvenile literature. [1. Festivals—New Zealand.
2. Holidays—New Zealand. 3. New Zealand—
Social life and customs.] I. Title. II. Series.
GT4893.A2G75   1999
394.26993—dc21   99-10858

1 2 3 4 5 6 7 8 9 03 02 01 00 99

CONTENTS

It's Festival Time . . .

New Zealanders love celebrations, and they really know how to have a good time! Besides national holidays, most little towns in New Zealand have their own local holidays as well. From sheep shearing and snowman building contests to flower festivals and *haka* [HAH-kuh] performances, New Zealanders are experts at creating excitement. Come, see for yourself—it's festival time in New Zealand!

WHERE'S NEW ZEALAND?

New Zealand is a group of islands in the southern Pacific Ocean. There are two main islands, North Island and South Island, and some other smaller islands. Its closest neighbor is Australia. New Zealand is very mountainous, particularly South Island. The country's capital city is Wellington.

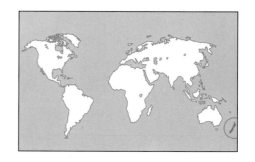

Who are the New Zealanders?

In the 10th century, the Maoris, from the South Pacific islands called Polynesia, settled in New Zealand. In the 19th century, Europeans arrived in New Zealand. They were mostly from Great Britain.

Today, about 10 percent of the population is Maori and 86 percent is of European descent. Modern New Zealand has the appearance of a European country, and the main language is English. Maori tradition, however, still forms an important part of New Zealand culture, and the Maori language is taught in some schools.

These children are of mixed Maori and European parentage.

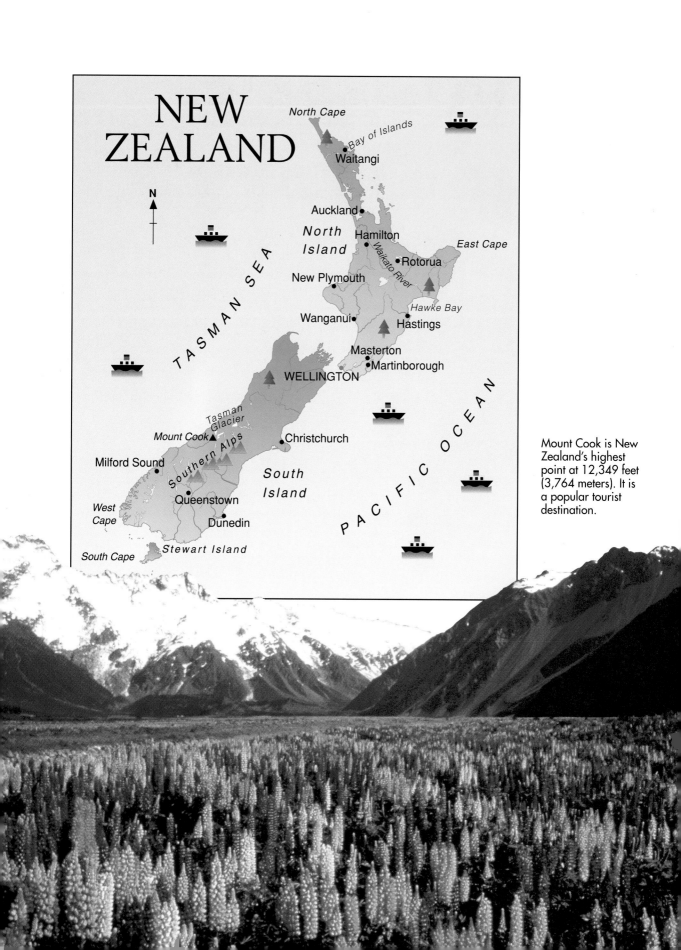

NEW ZEALAND

North Cape

Bay of Islands

Waitangi

N

Auckland

North Island

Hamilton

East Cape

TASMAN SEA

Rotorua

Waikato River

New Plymouth

Hawke Bay

Wanganui

Hastings

Masterton

Martinborough

WELLINGTON

Tasman Glacier

Mount Cook

Christchurch

Milford Sound

Southern Alps

South Island

PACIFIC OCEAN

Queenstown

West Cape

Dunedin

Stewart Island

South Cape

Mount Cook is New Zealand's highest point at 12,349 feet (3,764 meters). It is a popular tourist destination.

WHEN'S THE PARTY?

Do you know that there are more sheep than people in New Zealand? Join me for "shear" fun on pages 20–23!

New Zealand is located in the Southern Hemisphere, so its seasons are at opposite times of the year to countries in the Northern Hemisphere, such as the United States. When North Americans are dreaming of a white Christmas, New Zealanders are enjoying the blue skies of summer.

SUMMER

✪ **FESTIVAL OF LIGHTS**—New Plymouth and its surrounding areas celebrate the festive summer season from December 20th to February 8th by decorating streets and parks with lights.

✪ **CHRISTMAS DAY**

✪ **BOXING DAY**

✪ **NEW YEAR'S DAY**

✪ **INSTANT KIWI WORLD BUSKERS FESTIVAL**—Held in Christchurch in January, this is a week of entertainment by street performers from all over the world.

✪ **WAITANGI DAY**

✪ **MARTINBOROUGH FAIR**

✪ **CHRISTCHURCH FLOWER FESTIVAL**

✪ **AOTEAROA TRADITIONAL MAORI ARTS FESTIVAL**

AUTUMN

- ✪ **GOLDEN SHEARS**
- ✪ **NGARUAWAHIA REGATTA**—In March, traditional Maori entertainment complements canoe races on the Waikato River.
- ✪ **SCOTTISH WEEK**—In March, Dunedin celebrates the Scottish heritage of early settlers to that region.
- ✪ **EASTER**—Traditional Easter celebrations are combined with unique New Zealander events, such as Taihape Gumboot Day, which features a gumboot throwing competition!
- ✪ **ANZAC DAY**

WINTER

- ✪ **QUEEN'S BIRTHDAY**—This public holiday celebrates the birthday of New Zealand's head of state, the queen of England.
- ✪ **NATIONAL AGRICULTURAL FIELD DAYS**—Held in Hamilton in June, this event is one of the largest agricultural shows in the world.
- ✪ **CHRISTCHURCH ARTS FESTIVAL**—Held every two years, this mid-winter celebration features artists from New Zealand and overseas.
- ✪ **MOUNT COOK WINTER FESTIVAL**

SPRING

- ✪ **HASTINGS BLOSSOM FESTIVAL**—This festival celebrates the arrival of spring with a blossom parade through the streets of Hastings.
- ✪ **HERITAGE WEEK**—During this festival, New Zealanders celebrate the past and trace the developments of Christchurch.

Maori culture is a very important part of New Zealand history, and many holidays are devoted to Maori traditions. Read on to find out more!

NATIONAL HOLIDAYS

Waitangi Day and Anzac Day commemorate the two most significant events in New Zealand's history. Waitangi Day, or New Zealand day, is observed on February 6th every year. It celebrates the day New Zealand became a united nation, when the Maoris and the Europeans signed the Treaty of Waitangi in 1840.

Anzac Day honors all the valiant soldiers who have fought for their country and remembers those who died during the wars.

For many New Zealanders, Waitangi Day is a welcome summer holiday. It offers an opportunity to relax and enjoy a well-earned rest from school or work.

The Waitangi Treaty

When the first Europeans arrived in New Zealand in 1792, Maoris, the descendents of Polynesian settlers, had already been there for hundreds of years. They were protective of their land, and many conflicts arose between the European newcomers and the Maori people. Finally, on February 6, 1840, a treaty between Maori chiefs and the Europeans was established at Waitangi to end the fighting.

The signing of the Waitangi Treaty is celebrated all over New Zealand on Waitangi Day. At the site where the treaty was signed, the celebrations draw particularly large crowds. Both European and Maori people come to reenact the signing of the treaty, to put on traditional Maori performances, and to learn more about the foundation of their country.

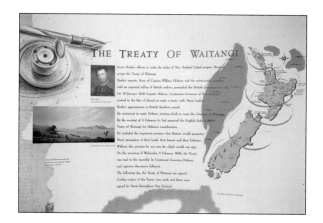

The Waitangi Treaty was signed by 50 Maori chiefs at Waitangi and, later, by more than 500 other chiefs around the country.

A war **veteran** pays his respects to fellow fallen soldiers at one of many memorial sites.

Anzac Day

ANZAC, or the Australian and New Zealand Army Corps, was formed during World War I. Anzac Day commemorates the bravery of New Zealand's armed forces in that war and those that followed.

The Anzac Day legend began at dawn on April 25, 1915, when New Zealand and Australian forces landed at Gallipoli on the coast of Turkey. They fought there against terrible odds, and thousands of lives were lost in the battle.

After the war, the ANZACs were honored for their bravery in the Gallipoli landing. The soldiers paraded through the streets of London and received honors from the king and queen of England.

Veterans with their war medals observe a solemn moment in the Anzac Day parade.

Remembering our heroes

Anzac Day is celebrated every year with parades and ceremonies that honor the courage of all soldiers who have fought for their country. On this day, dawn services are held throughout New Zealand to remember those who lost their lives in war, and a lone bugler plays *The Last Post*. Wreaths are laid at grave sites and memorials to fallen soldiers, and prayers are said for New Zealand's war heroes.

Parades are held all over the country on Anzac Day. Many New Zealanders line the streets as military and civilian bands march past, playing rousing music. War veterans march behind the bands, their war medals proudly displayed on their left breasts. A national service held in Wellington is attended by top military, government, and church officials, who join the people in honoring the ANZACs.

War veterans are honored on Anzac Day for their bravery in several wars.

Think about this

On Waitangi Day, many Maoris protest against the treatment of their people and the loss of their land since European settlement. The Maoris had been in New Zealand for hundreds of years before European settlement. Now, they are a minority group and have to fight hard for their rights. In recent years, however, many land rights issues have been settled peacefully. It is hoped that all conflicts between the groups will be settled soon.

SUMMER FUN

D uring the summer, many festivals are held throughout New Zealand to take advantage of the good weather. In Martinborough, a fair celebrating traditional English culture is held on February 7th. Christchurch holds a flower festival, with floral floats and beautiful floral displays.

The Martinborough Fair

The Martinborough Fair takes place around the village square, which comes alive with color and music as stalls and demonstrations compete for the attention of the crowds. Dances are very popular, local arts and crafts are displayed and sold, and the air is filled with the smells of foods being cooked. Children especially enjoy the rides that are offered as the fair gets into full swing.

Because Martinborough is not far from Wellington, the number of people who come to the fair is quite large. The crowds enjoy a traditional village fair that celebrates the way early European settlers to the country lived. Seafood, kiwifruit, and other delicious foods add a distinctly New Zealand touch to this event.

A typical New Zealand barbecue is a familiar sight at the Martinborough fair.

Opposite: Families gathered in a park await the start of a musical performance.

Christchurch, the "Garden City"

Christchurch is regarded by many people as New Zealand's most attractive city. It has many gardens, both public and private. In fact, gardening is the most popular pastime there, and the people of Christchurch are very proud of their gardens. It is no wonder, then, that their city is known as the "Garden City."

Tourists flock to Christchurch, especially in late summer, to see the incredible garden displays, skillfully landscaped and filled with beautiful flowers, such as chrysanthemums and geraniums.

This floral display is a beautiful **tribute** to music and nature.

Punts, or flat-bottomed boats pushed through the water with a long pole, are the best way to view the wonderful floral displays along the Avon River.

The Christchurch Flower Festival

The Christchurch Flower Festival is held every year from February 13th to the 22nd. During the festival, the beauty of Christchurch is enhanced with magnificent floral displays throughout the city. Highlights of the festival include floral floats on the Avon River and a 92-foot-long (28-meter-long) floral carpet down the aisle of Christchurch cathedral. Punts pick up people at designated landings and glide down the Avon River, so all can view the beautiful and creative floral floats.

Also during the festival, many private gardens are opened for display. At the Christchurch Festival, everyone can truly appreciate the beauty of New Zealand's "Garden City!"

The Christchurch Flower Festival showcases the talent and creativity of the townspeople in the beautiful floral displays they make with many different types of flowers.

Think about this

Many festivals and cultural events are held throughout New Zealand every year. Each little town has its own annual event in the form of a fair or a sporting competition. Does the town you live in organize a special event every year? What do you do at your festival?

Aotearoa Traditional Maori Arts Festival

Left: This Maori boy is doing his version of a war dance, called the haka.

Above: Maori girls perform with *poi* [POY], or soft balls attached to a string.

The Aotearoa Traditional Maori Arts Festival is one of the major cultural events in New Zealand. Aotearoa [AH-or-te-ah-roar], which means "land of the long white cloud," is the name the first Maori settlers gave their new home.

At the Aotearoa Festival, Maoris compete in traditional Maori arts contests, and the winners get to perform in other world competitions. The Aotearoa Festival has been held every two years since 1972, and it continues to grow as international interest increases. The festival is held in a different part of New Zealand each time, so it is a good way to promote Maori culture.

Kapa haka competitions

Over 30 groups perform at the Aotearoa Festival, after qualifying in smaller regional competitions. Each group, called *kapa haka* (KAH-puḥ HAH-kuh), competes by doing a haka unique to that group. Maori hakas often involve large groups of men and women.

The haka was traditionally performed before a battle or at the celebration of an event. A battle haka was scary, with face and body tattoos, loud voices, and foot stomping. It was meant to put fear into the hearts of the enemies.

Other performances at the festival are more gentle and celebrate the life and culture of the Maori. Maori women often dance with poi, twirling them in their hands as the haka is performed. Learning to dance with poi is a skill handed down through generations of Maori culture.

Above: Maori women can dazzle an audience with the poi dance.

Maoris greet each other by pressing their noses together. This greeting, called the **hongi** [HOR-ngee], is believed to connect the two people both physically and spiritually.

Maori crafts

The Aotearoa Festival offers an opportunity to learn more about Maori traditions and culture. For example, Maoris are famous for their wood carvings. During the festival, traditional Maori buildings are on display, filled with beautiful wood carvings. The large wooden pillars that support the buildings are carved with **intricate** patterns and designs, and the walls are often decorated with large woven panels called *tukutuku* (TOOK-oo TOOK-oo). All Maori buildings are decorated with artwork. A common feature is a figure known as the *tiki* (TEE-kee), which usually has a human shape with a large head—and an even larger tongue poking out! The tiki is very common throughout New Zealand; it is like an unofficial **mascot**. A *pare* (PAH-reh) is a wood carving with a combination of different designs. It normally decorates doorways and entrances.

A Maori craftsman adds the finishing touches to his wooden masterpiece.

The Maori meeting house is the center of all Maori activities. Notice the intricate designs and tiki figures carved along the beams and pillars of the building.

18

They came from the sea

While the main competition is going on, many other activities are offered at the Aotearoa Festival. One of the most popular is canoe racing. Maori canoes were once used in the ocean, as well as on rivers. The interest in canoe racing has helped keep the art of canoe building alive. The first Maori settlers came to New Zealand over the sea from other South Pacific islands. The vessel used for the journey is an important part of Maori lifestyle and culture.

    The Maori war canoe demonstrates the **ingenuity** of the early settlers. These canoes were not only beautiful, with intricately carved patterns, but they also were sturdy. They sometimes carried more than a hundred warriors at a time. The construction of the war canoe represents an incredible achievement of the Maoris.

Think about this

According to Maori legend, New Zealand was formed by the demigod Maui, who had fished North Island out of the sea with his magic fish hook. South Island was the canoe in which Maui was sitting when he caught his giant "fish," and Stewart Island was the anchor that held Maui's canoe. Do you know any myths that tell how your country was discovered or created?

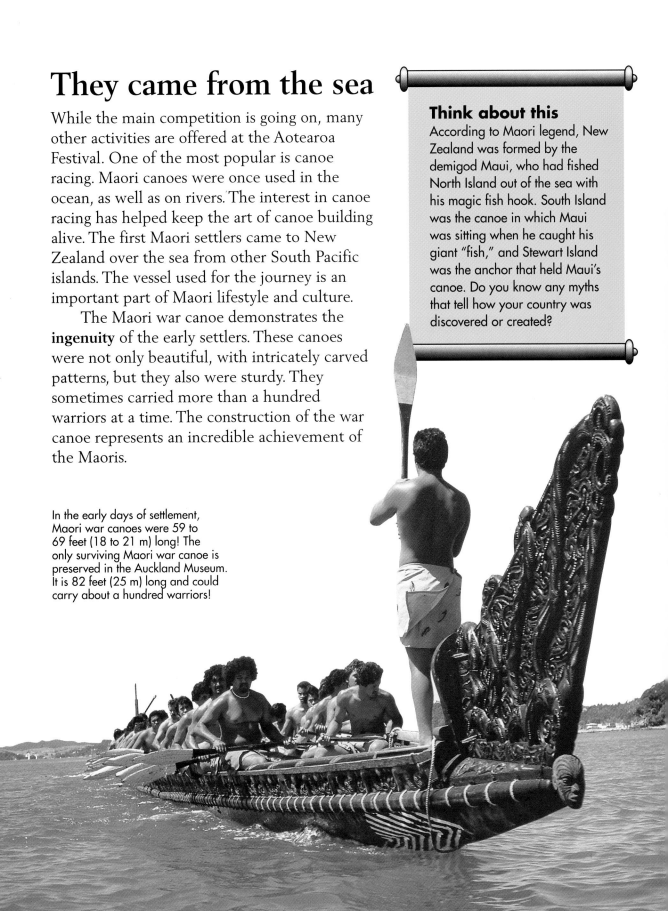

In the early days of settlement, Maori war canoes were 59 to 69 feet (18 to 21 m) long! The only surviving Maori war canoe is preserved in the Auckland Museum. It is 82 feet (25 m) long and could carry about a hundred warriors!

GOLDEN SHEARS

New Zealand is famous for its sheep, and wool farming is one of New Zealand's most important industries.

Golden Shears, held at Masterton, celebrates the place of sheep in New Zealand life. It showcases all the skills involved in raising sheep and producing fine-quality wool. Woolhandling competitions, including shearing and woolpressing, are exciting events in which shearers and woolhandlers demonstrate their skills. The ultimate prize for competitors is to become the supreme champion of Golden Shears.

The idea for this festival came in 1958, when a group of farmers organized a shearing contest. Three years later, Golden Shears was born, and it has since grown into one of the world's most famous agricultural events.

In New Zealand, there are more sheep than people—there are 14 sheep to every person!

A little girl proudly holds her lamb.

Shearing competitions

Shearing sheep is hard physical work that takes a lot of strength and concentration. Sheep shearers must not only be quick, but they must also be careful not to cut or injure the sheep. Expert shearers are in great demand. Sheep farmers depend on shearers who can shear their sheep quickly and cleanly.

When it is time for the best shearers to compete, large crowds gather in the woolsheds to watch. Many other competitions are held to demonstrate skills in other areas. There are demonstrations of sheep shearing the way it was done before electric shears were invented, and children can try shearing sheep, too. Most New Zealanders know how important the sheep industry is to their country, and they appreciate the skill involved in handling wool.

Sheep shearing competitions are the highlight of the Golden Shears festivities.

21

Sheepdogs and woolpressers

Sheepdog trials are another highlight of Golden Shears festivities. They are also one of the most popular pastimes in New Zealand, attracting large crowds and television audiences. In sheepdog trials, dogs are tested on their ability to make sheep do certain things, such as go through gates and into pens.

Sheepdogs are carefully bred for their skill in controlling flocks of sheep. Winning a trial can make a dog very valuable. Sheepdogs make a farmer's life a lot easier by keeping an eye on the sheep and making them go where the farmer needs them to be. For many farmers, the dogs are the most valuable workers on the farm—and they get paid only with food and pats!

Golden Shears also recognizes the work of woolpressers in the shearing sheds. In woolpressing competitions, contestants try to package as much wool as possible in the shortest amount of time.

Caring for lambs is a full-time job!

Sheepdog trials draw large crowds.

Counting sheep

Some farmers test their counting skills by competing against each other to see who can most accurately estimate the number of sheep in a pen or walking through a gate. Counting sheep is easy when there are not very many of them, but it gets harder when over a hundred sheep are involved. Some farmers, however, have been around sheep so long, they can tell how many sheep are standing in a pen just by looking at the flock.

Think about this

In New Zealand, sheep are raised for wool and meat. Every year, over 500 million tons of lamb and mutton are produced for local and overseas markets. Have you ever lived on a farm or visited one? What kinds of animals were raised on the farm? What products did these animals provide?

The world of sheep

Golden Shears has grown over the years, and, now, overseas competitors also participate in the competitions. Many competitors come from Australia, New Zealand's closest neighbor. New Zealanders, however, are difficult to beat when it comes to handling sheep, and they are proud of their skills. In fact, many New Zealand shearers work in Australia, and they like to show the Australians how it's done!

Counting sheep is easy for farmers who have lived on a sheep farm all their lives.

MOUNT COOK WINTER FESTIVAL

Mount Cook is New Zealand's highest point, at 12,349 feet (3,764 m), and the scene of one of the most exciting festivals in the country. Families throughout New Zealand come to the Mount Cook Winter Festival to enjoy the snow, spectacular scenery, and a variety of wintertime activities.

The Maoris call Mount Cook *Aorangi* [AH-or-rung-ee], which means "cloud piercer." You only have to stand in the valleys below Mount Cook and look up at the mountain to understand how appropriate this Maori name is. Read on to find out how New Zealanders have fun in the snow!

Enthusiastic young beginners pose on a ski slope.

Fun in the snow

July is the middle of winter in New Zealand. It is also the time to enjoy the Mount Cook Winter Festival, with its many skiing competitions and other winter events. Some of the competitions are spectacular to watch. In freestyle competitions, for example, competitors perform tricks and somersaults on their skis. Other contests are more for fun, such as ski races with skiers in fancy dress.

Building snowmen is always popular with children, so the Mount Cook Winter Festival features a snowman building competition. Some contestants take this event very seriously and try to build bigger and better snowmen each time. Some just have fun throwing snowballs at each other!

At night, it is traditional to gather around a big fire and enjoy the winter landscape of Mount Cook.

An ice sculpting competition adds to the excitement of a winter festival.

Skiing competitions highlight the festivities at Mount Cook.

THINGS FOR YOU TO DO

The Maoris have a very rich culture. One of the more striking features of their culture is the tradition of tattooing whole bodies and faces. The Maoris also use a number of chants and songs to celebrate or prepare for special occasions. The most famous of these is the haka, a fierce challenge chanted by warriors before a battle. It must have been a truly scary sight to see tattooed Maori warriors holding spears and chanting the haka! You can paint your face and learn the haka just like a Maori warrior!

Fun with tattoo!

The practice of tattooing comes from the Polynesian people, who, thousands of years ago, settled in the islands now known as New Zealand. You can tattoo your face, too. All you need are water-based face paints, preferably the colors green and black.

Look through this book or other books about New Zealand for a picture of a Maori with a tattooed face, such as the one on the left, and copy the tattoo pattern. Start by outlining your face with the paint. Then add scrolled or curved patterns within the outline, following the contours of your face. The lines should be about 0.5 inch (1 centimeter) wide. When you think you look fierce enough, you are ready to do the haka.

Learn the haka!

The haka is an important cultural element of New Zealand life. Although it is specifically Maori, it is performed with great pride by both white and Maori members of the national rugby team. The men chant the haka loudly and defiantly, slapping their thighs and bodies and sticking out their tongues. You can learn the haka, too! Chant the lines below loudly as you slap your thighs and stick out your tongue.

Ka mate Ka mate [KUH MAH-tay KUH MAH-tay]
Ka ora Ka ora [KUH o-RUH KUH o-RUH]
(Repeat the first two lines.)
Tenei Te Tangata Puhuruhuru [te-NAY TAY tahn-GAH-tah POO-hoo-roo-HOO-roo]
Nana i tiki mai whakawhiti te ra [nah-NAH EE TEE-kee MAY WUCK-uh-WEE-tee TEE RAH]
Upane Upane [UP-ah-NEE UP-ah-NEE]
Whiti te ra [wit-EE TAY RAH]

Translation:
It is death, it is death.
It is life, it is life.
(Repeat the first two lines.)
This is the hairy man
Who caused the sun to shine again for me.
Up the ladder. Up the ladder.
Up to the top…
The sun shines!

Things to look for in your library

A Home by the Sea: Protecting Coastal Wildlife. Kenneth Mallory (Gulliver Books, 1998).
Maori. Threatened Cultures (series). Robert MacDonald (Thomson Learning, 1994).
New Zealand. Cultures of the World (series). Roselynn Smelt (Marshall Cavendish Corporation, 1998).
New Zealand Shake-up. Stacy Towle Morgan (Bethany House Publishers, 1997).
Passport to New Zealand. (http://www.nztb.govt.nz/).
Sir Edmund Hillary: To Everest and Beyond. Newsmakers (series). Whitney Stewart and Anne B. Keiser (Lerner Publications Company, 1995).
Touring New Zealand. (Questar Inc., 1998).

MAKE A PARE

The Maori use woven panels and wooden carvings to decorate their homes, meeting houses, and other buildings. A pare is a long wooden carving used to decorate the entrance of a Maori dwelling. It normally depicts a series of tiki figures, or characters with big heads, large eyes, and long tongues. Follow these steps to make your own Maori pare!

You will need:
1. White cardboard, 12" x 22" (30 cm x 56 cm)
2. Ruler
3. Black and red paint
4. Paintbrushes
5. Pencil
6. Paint tray

1 Copying the Maori designs below, draw a few tiki figures along the length of the cardboard.

2 Paint the figures. Paint straight lines and V-shaped designs on the bodies. Paint red and black curved lines around the eyes and the outline of the face. Paint in the pupils of the eyes. Give each tiki figure a different expression by varying the position of the pupils in the eyes. Paint the tongues red. When the paint is dry, place your pare above a door. According to Maori legend, the pare will keep out unwanted guests!

MAKE KIWI-MANGO SORBET

New Zealand's most famous fruit is kiwifruit. It is rich in vitamin C and is used a lot in New Zealand cooking. Sorbet is a delicious icy treat that is easy to make. Follow these simple steps to make a refreshing kiwi treat!

You will need:
1. Blender
2. Square cake pan
3. 1 can of mango slices
4. 6 kiwifruit, peeled and sliced
5. 1 tablespoon of fresh orange juice
6. Spoon
7. Measuring spoons

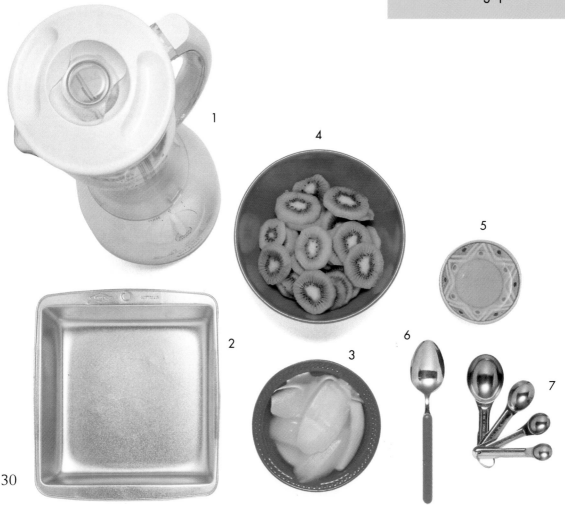

1
4
5
2
3
6
7

1 Blend the kiwifruit, the mango slices (including the syrup in the can), and the orange juice to make a puree.

2 Pour the mixture into the cake pan and freeze it for about an hour, until ice crystals start to form.

3 Blend the icy mixture. Then pour it back into the cake pan and freeze it. Place scoops of the frozen sorbet into dessert bowls and serve it with slices of kiwifruit. Now you have a refreshing and cool dessert!

GLOSSARY

hongi, 17 — The traditional Maori greeting of pressing noses together, which is believed to join people in body and spirit.

implemented, 9 — Accomplished or put into effect.

ingenuity, 19 — Originality, intelligence, or skill at inventing new things.

intricate, 18 — Complex and detailed.

mascot, 18 — A person, animal, or symbol adopted by an organization or event for good luck or to serve as a representative.

pare, 18 — A long, wooden carving used to decorate the entrance of a Maori building.

tiki, 18 — A human figure commonly found in Maori carvings, which represents a Maori god or an ancestor.

tribute, 14 — Something said, written, or made to show respect, honor, admiration, or praise for someone or something.

veteran, 10 — A person who has served his or her country in the armed forces, especially during a war.

INDEX

Picture credits
Oliver Bolch: 28; Susanna Burton: 3 (top), 7 (top), 8, 10 (both), 11, 12, 13; Camera Press: 23; Focus Team/Italy: 21 (bottom); Blaine Harrington: 7 (bottom), 18 (top), 20 (top), 21 (top); The Hutchison Library: 26; Kanga Concepts: 14 (both), 15; New Zealand Tourism Board: 2, 3 (bottom), 5, 6, 16 (both), 17 (both), 22 (top), 24, 25 (both), 27 (both); David Simson: 1, 4, 9 (bottom); Topham Picture Point: 18 (bottom); Trip Photographic Library: 9 (top), 19, 20 (bottom), 22 (bottom)

Digital scanning by
Superskill Graphics Pte Ltd.